THE RETURN OF THE ANTELOPE

Pictures by FAITH JAQUES

BASED ON THE GRANADA TELEVISION SERIES
By WILLIS HALL

Picture Book Text by MARY HOFFMAN

Puffin Books

The Return of the Antelope is a 13-part Granada
Television series directed by Eugene Ferguson.

Lilliput

*The country of Lilliput was invented more than two hundred
years ago by Jonathan Swift in his book* Gulliver's Travels.
*Gulliver was ship-wrecked on the coast of Lilliput, a land of
tiny people. That was in the year 1699. In Willis Hall's story,
three people from Lilliput come to England in the year 1899.*

It was the last day of the holidays. It had been cold and wet all summer and Gerald and Philippa were miserable. They hated the boarding-house where they were staying with their grandfather – the landlady was always cross, and wouldn't let them do anything.

There had been a terrible storm the night before.

"Let's go down to the beach for the last time," said Gerald. "Perhaps the storm has washed up something interesting."

So off they went.

"Why, there's a boat!" cried Philippa. "It's been wrecked in the storm."

"But it's much too small to be a real boat," said Gerald. "You couldn't get a person in that."

"It's even got a name – the *Antelope*," said Philippa. "And look! There are the crew!"

Standing on the beach were three tiny people, shouting and waving their arms.

"Oh, what dears!" said Philippa. "Who do you suppose they can be?" She tried to pick one up, but he struggled frantically.

"If you let us take you home with us we can help you," said Gerald. "You must be cold and hungry."

The three little people whispered together, then nodded.

The children carried them back to the boarding-house. Gerald and Philippa were very excited.

"It'll be a secret," said Philippa. "We won't tell any grown-ups."

They didn't know it but a grown-up was watching them at that very moment. He was Harwell Mincing, the landlady's brother. As the children carried the little people upstairs, their captain dropped his dagger. Harwell Mincing picked it up.

"This little dagger is too sharp to be a toy," he said. "It stands to reason that it must belong to a very small person indeed. I wonder what those children know about it."

Gerald and Philippa took the three little sailors into their bedroom.
"Now, tell us who you are," said Gerald.

First there was Spelbush. He was the leader. "I have come all the way from Lilliput to see if your country is real," he said. "I demand that you giants take me to your Emperor!"

Then there was Brelca, a brave woman sailor. She said, "I have sailed over seven oceans in the *Antelope*. All but three of us were drowned. The least we deserve is a hero's welcome. And I'd like some new clothes too."

Last was Fistram. He was really the easiest to please. "Just be sure you remember to feed us," he said. "We are grown-up people, even though we are so much smaller than you. We can't live on milk and biscuits."

The children kept their secret well. The next morning they smuggled the little people downstairs in their luggage. Grandfather was in a hurry to catch the train back to town.

The landlady and her brother were waiting to see them off.

"Goodbye, dear children," said Harwell Mincing. "I hope we meet again. Let me give you my card."

"'Mincing's Fairground Freaks'," read Gerald. "What's this?"

"It's my little show," said Harwell Mincing. "You must come and see it one day."

When they were safely out of the house Gerald whispered to Spelbush, "You see, we *must* keep you hidden. If Mincing gets hold of you, you'll be put on show like a bearded lady!"

Back home, Gerald and Philippa rushed up to the nursery and put the little people in the doll's house.

"There, isn't that a nice house for you?" cried Philippa.

But the little people didn't like it.

"It's all pretend," said Spelbush.

"Just painted on," complained Brelca.

"Not real," agreed Fistram.

"How ungrateful they are," Philippa whispered to Gerald.

"It's the best place for you, you know," said Gerald.

"I suppose it'll do for the time being," said Spelbush. "But you can't expect us to stay here for ever."

The children soon found it was much harder keeping their secret than they had imagined. Millie the maid was always in and out of the nursery. She was very interested in the doll's house. Whenever she looked in through the window, Spelbush, Fistram and Brelca had to pretend to be dolls.

"Ooh, don't they look *real*!" Millie said.

It wasn't just Millie they had to worry about. The little people wouldn't stay in the doll's house: they wanted to explore the nursery. Brelca nearly got shut in a drawer. Fistram fell into some blancmange, and Spelbush got sucked into the new vacuum cleaner. The children had to give them three meals a day and even had to make new clothes.

"It's much worse than when we had tadpoles," grumbled Philippa.

But it wasn't difficult all the time. It was a marvellous secret to have three little people no higher than a milk-jug living in their own house. And sometimes they could be useful. When Gerald and Philippa didn't feel like doing their piano practice, Fistram and Brelca could run and jump over the keys for them. It sounded just like real music.

Gerald read to them from *Gulliver's Travels*. The little people thought it was very funny.

"He got it all wrong, you know," said Spelbush.

Soon there was a new problem. The crew of the *Antelope* were used to an open-air life and they got tired of being cooped up indoors. At first they sat in the window-box. It was just like a garden for them. But later they wanted to go right outside the house and explore.

One day the children took them out into the real garden. Spelbush had to get out his sword to cut through the grass. Brelca met a giant spider. Fistram climbed onto a mushroom and started nibbling.

"This is awful," said Gerald. "I'm sure one of them will be attacked by a blackbird."

"Or get lost in the weeds," said Philippa.

But the people from Lilliput were quite happy.

Suddenly Philippa said, "Someone's coming!" She snatched up the little people into her pinafore pocket.

"It's the new gardener," said Gerald. "I don't like the look of him. In fact, he reminds me of Harwell Mincing."

"That's it! It's Harwell Mincing in disguise!" said Philippa. "He's come to get them for his show. Quick let's take them into the summerhouse."

Philippa was right. Harwell Mincing had guessed they were hiding the little people and had followed the children home. He was determined to catch them.

"Whatever is he doing?" asked Brelca.

"Looks as if he's setting traps," said Fistram.

"Well, they'd better not be for us," said Spelbush fiercely.

But they were! The little people were horrified when they heard Harwell Mincing say to himself, "Roll up, roll up, see the world's smallest people! Just wait till I catch you, my little dears, I'll be rich, rich, rich!"

And he went on pegging out the netting.

"We'll have to stay in the summerhouse till he's gone," said Fistram.

"I'm not going to hide!" said Brelca fiercely. "I know how to frighten him off for good and all. Come with me!"

When the children weren't looking, they crept out of the summerhouse and across the lawn. Harwell Mincing couldn't see them in the long grass. They found a coal-hole with the lid off and dragged a sack over it. Then Brelca and Spelbush put an empty flower-pot on top of Fistram. While he walked up and down behind the coal-hole, the other two shouted as loudly as they could.

"What's that noise?" said Harwell Mincing. He looked up just as Brelca and Spelbush scurried behind the watering can. "I do believe they're here in the garden already!"

Then he saw the flower pot move.

"That must be one of them! How else could a flower pot move?" he cried. "By George, I'm going to catch them."

He ran towards the flower pot, without noticing the sack.

Hearing Mincing's cries from the cellar, the children rushed to scoop up the three little people and carry them safely upstairs.

"*He* won't be back in a hurry," said Spelbush, as they looked out of the window and watched Mincing running away.

"The cheek of it," said Brelca. "Fancy wanting to put *us* in his fairground show! Back in Lilliput we'd put *him* on show for a giant — just like Gulliver."

Fistram said nothing. He was unusually quiet. So Gerald read them all a bit more of *Gulliver's Travels*.

That night Gerald and Philippa sat up late talking.

"It's no good, Philly," said Gerald. "It's too hard keeping them safe. We'll either have to tell a grown-up, or let them go."

"But where would they go?" said Philippa. "They'd be trodden on the minute they left the house."

"We're stuck with them," said Gerald gloomily. "But I don't think they're safe here any more. And I don't care what Spelbush says. That man Mincing will be back."

A few days later when the children were having breakfast, it was Fistram who solved the problem. Usually he was the hungriest, but today he just sat in Philippa's saucer, with his head in his hands.

"Come on, Fistram, buck up," said Brelca. "This isn't like you. Why back home in Lilliput you sometimes eat six eggs for breakfast!"

Fistram burst into tears.

"Is something the matter?" asked Philippa.

"All this talk of Lilliput," he sobbed. "I want to go *home!*"

"What about you two?" Gerald asked the others.

Spelbush and Brelca looked embarrassed. The children could tell that they wanted to go back to Lilliput too.

"But how are we to get there?" asked Spelbush. "The *Antelope* was smashed to bits and we'll never find another ship as good as her or the right size for us."

Gerald and Philippa turned out their toy cupboard to find something suitable. They had two toy boats but neither of them was good enough for the crew of the *Antelope*.

"That's not a proper ship," said Spelbush to Gerald. "You see it's made of solid wood below. There's nowhere for us to sleep."

"Remember it's got to cross seven oceans," said Brelca. "It's not like sailing on a duck-pond, you know."

"And we must have somewhere to store all our food," said Fistram, who was much more cheerful now that they were making plans for going home.

It seemed impossible to find something small enough that would still be a proper ship, but one day the children had a piece of luck. In the window of the shipping line they saw a beautiful model of a sailing ship, just the right size.

"That would be perfect," said Gerald. "Let's ask if we can buy it."

"We could never afford it," said Philippa.

But it just happened that the shipping line were changing over to steam-ships. So they didn't need the model of the sailing ship any more.

"You can have it for nothing," said the man in the shop.

The sailors from Lilliput were overjoyed.
"This is much more like it," said Spelbush.
They all explored the ship.

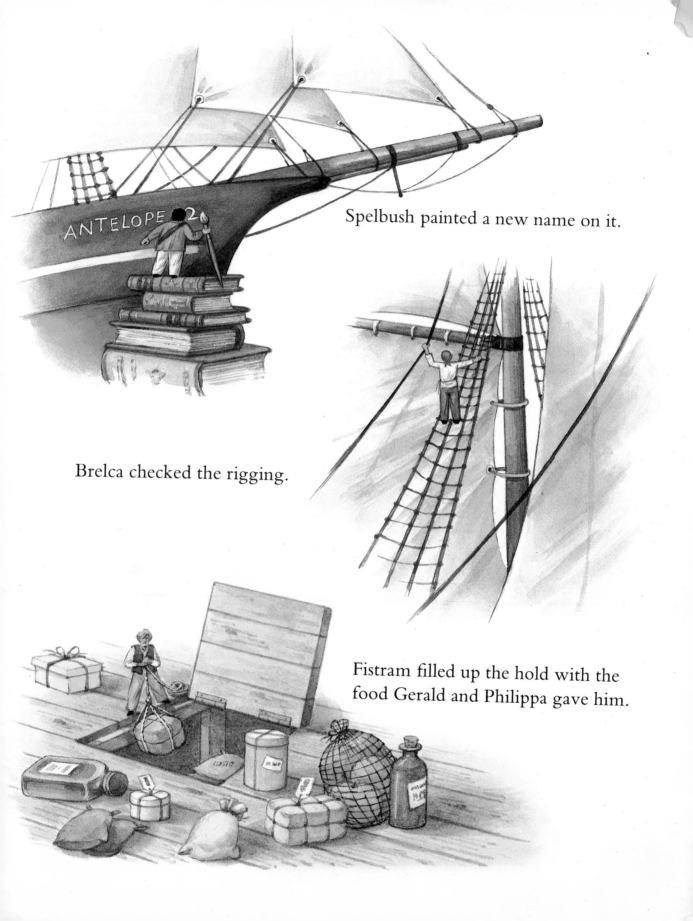

Spelbush painted a new name on it.

Brelca checked the rigging.

Fistram filled up the hold with the food Gerald and Philippa gave him.

When everything was ready, Gerald and Philippa gently carried the *Antelope 2* and its crew to the river bank.

"This will take you down to the coast where you were shipwrecked," said Gerald.

"Where we found you," said Philippa.

Now that the little people from Lilliput were leaving, the children were both sad. It had been the best secret they had ever had.

"Farewell," said Spelbush. "On behalf of my crew, may I express my gratitude to you for your hospitality?"

"He means thank you for having us," said Brelca.

"Thank you for coming," said Gerald.

"Goodbye," said Fistram. "We'll never forget you – or the blancmange."

"Goodbye," said Philippa. "We'll never forget you either."

And so the three little people the children had kept secret for so long sailed down the river, waving goodbye.

"They were very nice children," said Brelca, "even though they were giants."

"Very helpful children," said Spelbush, "even though they never did take us to their Emperor."

"Very kind children," said Fistram, who was looking sad again.

"Come on," said Brelca, "you can't start feeling homesick for Gerald and Philippa now. We're going home to Lilliput!"

But a lot can happen when you have seven oceans to cross. And they were still a long way from Lilliput.